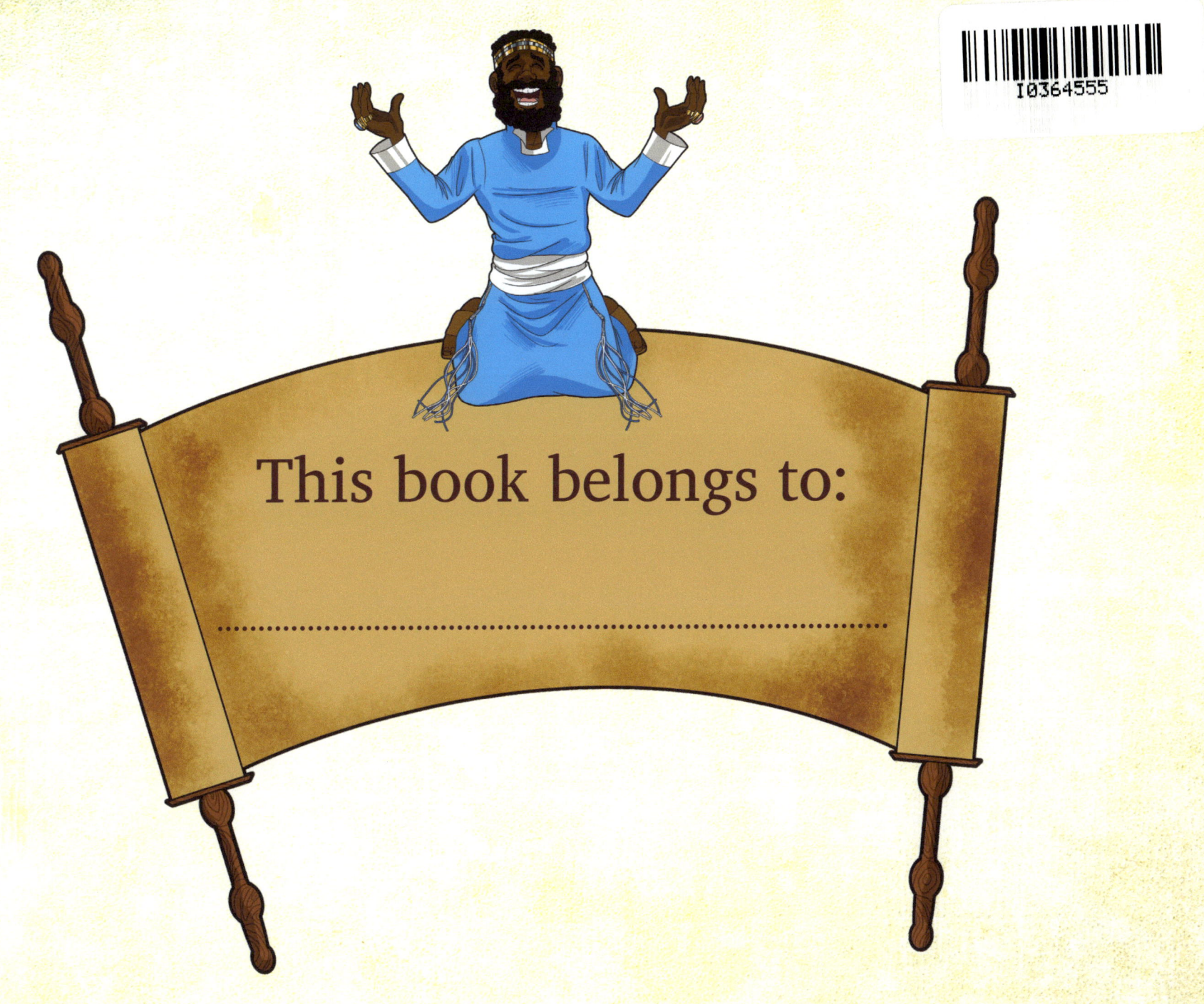

This book belongs to:

....

Copyright © BPA Publishing Ltd 2020

Author: Pip Reid
Illustrator: Thomas Barnett
Creative Director: Curtis Reid

www.biblepathwayadventures.com

Thank you for supporting Bible Pathway Adventures®. Our adventure series helps parents teach their children more about the Bible in a fun creative way. Designed for the whole family, Bible Pathway Adventures' mission is to help bring discipleship back into homes around the world. The search for truth is more fun than tradition!

The moral rights of author and illustrator have been asserted, this book is copyright.

ISBN: 978-1-989961-05-6

King Solomon

The Temple Builder

"I have built a magnificent temple for You, a place for You to dwell forever." (1 Kings 8:13)

In the time when kings ruled the land of Israel, there lived a brave king named David. He loved God with all his heart and ruled fairly over the people. As he grew older, the people wondered, *Who will be the next king of Israel?*

"Our son Solomon will be crowned king after me," David said to his wife, Bathsheba. Little did they know that the eldest son – a man named Adonijah -- was plotting to take over the kingdom.

Bathsheba soon found out about Adonijah's plans. She hurried to see David. "You promised me that Solomon would be the next king," she cried. "But Adonijah has got himself chariots and horsemen. He is making himself king."

Just then, the prophet Nathan rushed into the room. "You and your son Solomon are in great danger," he said. "The people are cheering for Adonijah. You must tell everyone who will be the king after you." David frowned. He had to act fast! "Quickly!" he said to Nathan. "Put Solomon on my donkey. Go down to Gihon Spring and anoint him as king. Solomon will be the next king of Israel."

Nathan wasted no time. He put Solomon on a donkey and took him to Gihon Spring. There, Solomon knelt down before the people. The high priest took a horn of olive oil and poured it over Solomon's head. "You are now the next king of Israel," he said.

The Israelites clapped and cheered, and the shofars blared. "Long live King Solomon! Long live the king!" they sang. They followed Solomon into the city, playing their instruments and shouting for joy.

The news about Solomon spread quickly across Jerusalem. In no time, it had reached the ears of Adonijah's friends. Their faces turned pale and their knees knocked with fear. They had cheered for the wrong king! Adonijah was scared, too. Solomon might kill him for what he had done. But he had nothing to worry about. Solomon had mercy on him and let him live.

While King David was still alive, he made plans to build a temple in Jerusalem. But God did not allow David to build it himself. "You have been a man of war," He said, "and I want a man of peace. Your son Solomon will build the temple."

David gave Solomon plans for building the temple. They included plans for its buildings, its storerooms, its inside rooms, and the Most Holy Place. Solomon marvelled at all the treasure his father had stored, including piles of gold and silver, marble and precious stones. "Use this treasure to build the temple," said David. "Do not let anyone stop you."

Before he died, David gave Solomon some final instructions. "Remember to obey God's commandments," he said. "If you do, your life will go well. But if you disobey them, you will have many problems."

Did you know?

While David was king, his son Absalom tried to overthrow him and become king. Absalom was killed in a battle against his father (2 Samuel 18).

After the death of David, Solomon began to rule the kingdom. But there was just one problem. Adonijah still wanted to be king. He said to Bathsheba, "I know Solomon will do whatever you say. Tell him I want to take Abishag of Shunem as my wife." Abishag had cared for David before he died, and kept him warm.

Solomon was angry. If Adonijah married David's caretaker, it would show the people that Adonijah should be king. "My brother wants to take over the kingdom!" shouted Solomon. He thumped the throne with his fist. "I swear he will die today."

Solomon called for Benaiah, the captain of his bodyguards. "I have no choice," he said. "Adonijah cannot be king. Now kill him!" **Thadump thadump, thadump**. With his sword in his hand, Benaiah marched out of the palace to find Adonijah.

While he was king, Solomon often visited the high place at Gibeon to worship and pray. One day, he went there to offer sacrifices to God. In the night he had a dream. God came to him and said, "What can I give you?" Solomon remembered how God had helped his father, David. He said, "Give me wisdom to rule the people, and to know the difference between good and evil."

God was happy with Solomon's answer. "Because you have asked for great wisdom instead of riches and power," God said, "I will give you more wisdom than anyone else. You will have riches and honor all your life. You will be the greatest king in the world. And if you obey Me and keep My Torah, I will give you a long life."

Solomon was filled with joy. He jumped out of bed and hurried back to Jerusalem. There he offered even more sacrifices to God. Then he held a big party at the palace that lasted all day and all night.

King Solomon became known everywhere for his great wisdom. One day, two mothers came to his palace with a problem. The first said, "This woman and I live in the same house. I had a baby boy and so did she. Her baby died and now she says my baby is hers."

"No!" shouted the other woman. "The living child is mine and the dead one is yours." Solomon held up his hand to silence the women. He thought for a moment. "Cut the child in half with a sword," he said. "Each of you may have half of the baby."

As Solomon's servant reached for the sword, the real mother cried out. "Please don't kill my child," she said. "Give the baby to her." The other woman said, "Don't give the baby to either of us. Cut it in two!" Solomon stood to his feet. "Stop!" he said. "Don't kill the baby." He pointed to the first woman. "Give him to her. She is the real mother." When the Israelites heard about Solomon's wise decision, they greatly respected the king. They saw he had the wisdom of God to make good decisions.

While Solomon was king, he built many buildings, including a palace in Jerusalem for himself. But the most famous place he built was God's temple. Building the temple was a big job. Solomon needed 80,000 men to cut stones for the foundations, and 70,000 men to carry them. He wrote a letter to King Hiram from the nearby city of Tyre, which was by the sea.

The message said, "Now that we have peace, I will build a temple to worship God. Give me your beautiful cedar trees, and I will pay your men and send my men to help."

King Hiram was happy to help. "My men will cut down as many trees as you need," he said. His servants tied the logs together to make rafts and floated them down the coast to the land of Israel. In return, Solomon sent wheat and olive oil to help the king feed his men.

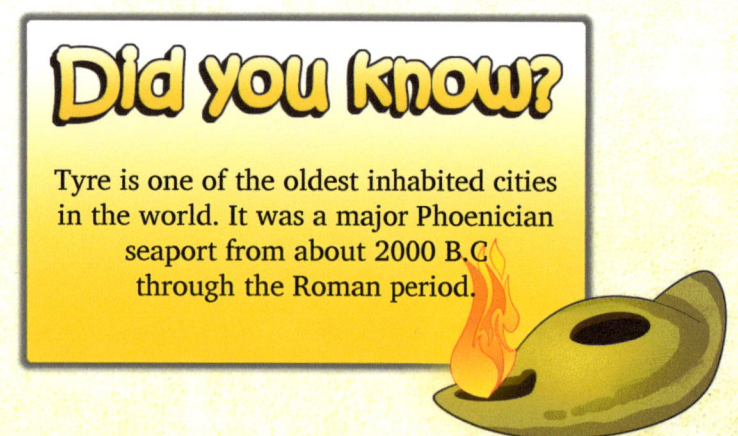

Did you know?

Tyre is one of the oldest inhabited cities in the world. It was a major Phoenician seaport from about 2000 B.C. through the Roman period.

For seven years, Solomon's men worked – sawing, cutting and carving – to build the temple. The stones were cut in quarries away from the temple, so that no hammer, axe, or iron tool was heard at the temple site while it was being built.

Inside the temple, the walls were made of fine wood, covered in gold. All of the furnishings and vessels for worship were also made of gold. Solomon built a room at the back of the temple called the Most Holy Place. This was for the Ark of the Covenant, a gold box that held the two precious stone tablets on which God had written His commandments.

When the work was finished, Solomon brought everything his father had set aside for the temple – the gold and silver, stones and marble – and put them into rooms at the temple. Now God had a house where His people could worship Him. "This house is beautiful," said Solomon. He could hardly wait to dedicate the temple to God.

Did you know?

The temple was built like the Tabernacle in the wilderness. It was divided into three areas: the Most Holy Place, the Holy Place and the outer courtyard.

During the seventh month, the men of Israel came to Jerusalem to celebrate the Fall Feasts. The city was filled with people talking and praying and asking questions. They camped outside the city walls in a maze of tents. Everyone was excited to honor the Feasts!

In a special ceremony, Solomon dedicated the temple to God. The Levites carried the Ark of the Covenant from its tent to the Most Holy Place. Priests blew the shofars and the people started singing: "God is good. His love will last forever!"

Suddenly, the temple was filled with a thick cloud. It was the glory of God. Solomon stretched his arms to the sky. "My father wanted to build this temple," he said. "But God told him that I shall build it. So I have built a temple where His name can live forever." Then, fire came down from the sky like a thunderbolt. All the offerings were burnt to blackened ashes.

That week, the Israelites celebrated at the temple. They sang and danced and played their tambourines. It was like a great wedding feast for seven days! They were happy because of all the good things that God had done for His people Israel.

God kept His promise to make Solomon the greatest king in the world. His kingdom grew bigger and bigger. He ruled over all the nations from the Euphrates River in the north, to Egypt in the south.

But Solomon wanted to be king of the seas. With help from King Hiram, he built a fleet of ships near the Red Sea. Soon his men were sailing all over the world to trade with other countries and make new friends.

Every three years, the men came home with gifts for the king. They brought gold and silver, ivory and apes, and even peacocks. Solomon used these gifts to decorate the huge royal palace he had built for himself.

Did you know?

The Los Lunas Stone discovered in New Mexico has the Ten Commandments engraved in ancient Hebrew script, dated to 1,000 B.C

Far away from the land of Israel, there lived a queen who ruled the kingdom of Sheba. She had heard all about Solomon's wisdom and his friendship with God. The queen made up her mind to visit the king. "Pack my camels," she said to her servants. "I want to meet this king and hear his wisdom for myself."

The servants were quick to obey the queen's orders. They loaded a caravan of camels with gold, spices, and precious stones, and set out for Jerusalem.

It was a long trip, a few thousand miles, through the desert. Every day, the sun beat down dusty and hot. At night when it became cold and dark, bright stars lit their way to Jerusalem. The queen had to be careful. Fearsome bandits waited in the darkness looking for caravans to rob. It was a long and dangerous journey.

Did you know?

A group of camels is called a caravan. Camels have three sets of eyelids and two rows of eyelashes to keep sand out of their eyes.

One evening, the camels finally stopped outside the king's palace. The queen had arrived in Jerusalem. Solomon met her in his throne room. *"Bruchim haba'im Le Yerushalaim!"* he said. "Welcome to Jerusalem!" The queen stared around the room, wide-eyed. Twelve golden lions guarded the throne. Enormous wooden pillars rose high in the air. "So many servants! Such fine clothing!" she whispered. "I did not believe these things until I saw them myself."

Solomon held a great feast for the queen. Food, wine, and music filled the palace. The musicians played their instruments, and everyone ate and drank until they were full. Afterward, the queen asked Solomon many hard questions. But there was not even one question he could not answer. His wisdom had come from God.

"What I heard in my own country about you is true," said the queen. "You are richer and wiser than I imagined. Praise God who made you king of the Israelites." She gave Solomon many gifts, including more spices than he had ever seen. And he gave her whatever her heart desired.

While he was king, Solomon wrote many songs and wise sayings. These were known as proverbs. Because the proverbs were from God, they were true and full of wisdom. Solomon wrote proverbs like:

"Obey your father's command and do not forget your mother's teaching."

"Trust in God with all your heart; do not rely on your own understanding. In all your ways acknowledge Him and He will direct your paths."

"He who is generous is blessed because he shares his food with the poor."

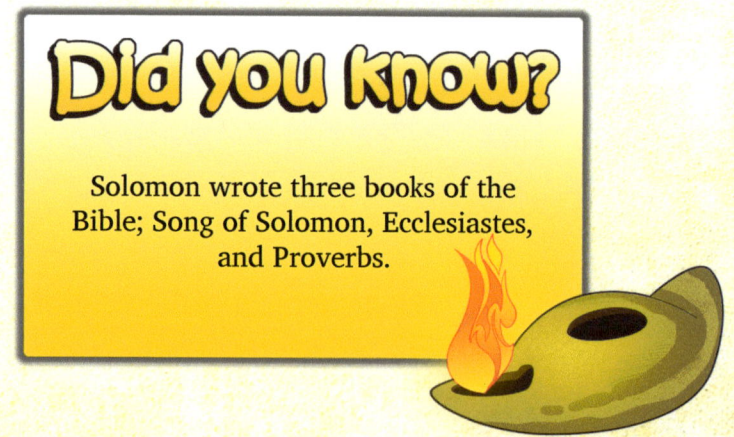

Did you know?

Solomon wrote three books of the Bible; Song of Solomon, Ecclesiastes, and Proverbs.

Solomon was a wise king. But he didn't always listen to God. He ignored God's instructions not to marry foreign women or follow their ways. At first, he married Pharaoh's daughter. And then he married another. Soon he had hundreds of wives. Every day they bowed down and prayed to their false gods.

To keep his wives happy, Solomon built altars on top of hills so they could worship their idols. He built them places to worship Chemosh, the god of Moab, and shrines to worship Molech, the god of the Ammonites. Solomon's heart turned away from God and he began to worship these gods, too.

God was not pleased with Solomon. "You have taught the people to worship idols instead of Me," He said. "For this, I will tear your kingdom into two pieces and give it to one of your servants. But for your father's sake, I will wait until you are dead."

Did you know?

Solomon had 700 wives and 300 concubines (1 Kings 11:3). Many of them came from other countries and led him away from God.

In the meantime, servants like Jeroboam were sent to weaken Solomon's kingdom. One day as Jeroboam was leaving Jerusalem, he saw the prophet Ahijah alone on the road. God had sent Ahijah to warn Jeroboam that he was going to judge Israel.

Ahijah took off the new robe he was wearing, and ripped it into twelve pieces. "Take ten pieces of the robe for yourself," he said to Jeroboam. "Because Solomon has tried to worship God and idols, God will take the kingdom away from his sons and give it to you. Solomon's sons will rule over two tribes of Israel; the other ten tribes are for you."

When Solomon heard what Ahijah had said, he was angry. "Find Jeroboam and kill him!" he shouted. But Jeroboam escaped to Egypt where he could not be found.

During the last days of Solomon's reign, things did not go well. He did not listen to the people's troubles. Soon there was no peace in the kingdom. As Solomon turned away from God, the tribes turned against Solomon. God sent many enemies to attack him.

After Solomon died, his son Rehoboam became king. But the tribes caused even more trouble. The kingdom was split into two parts; Israel and Judah. Each part had its own king. Rehoboam became the king of Judah, while Jeroboam ruled ten of the tribes of Israel.

The tribes grew more wicked and turned against God. He punished them by sending them out of the land. They were scattered over all the earth. Everything happened just as God had said.

Because Solomon's heart had turned away from God, the nation of Israel was judged. Even a king with great wisdom needs to love and honor God's Ways.

THE END

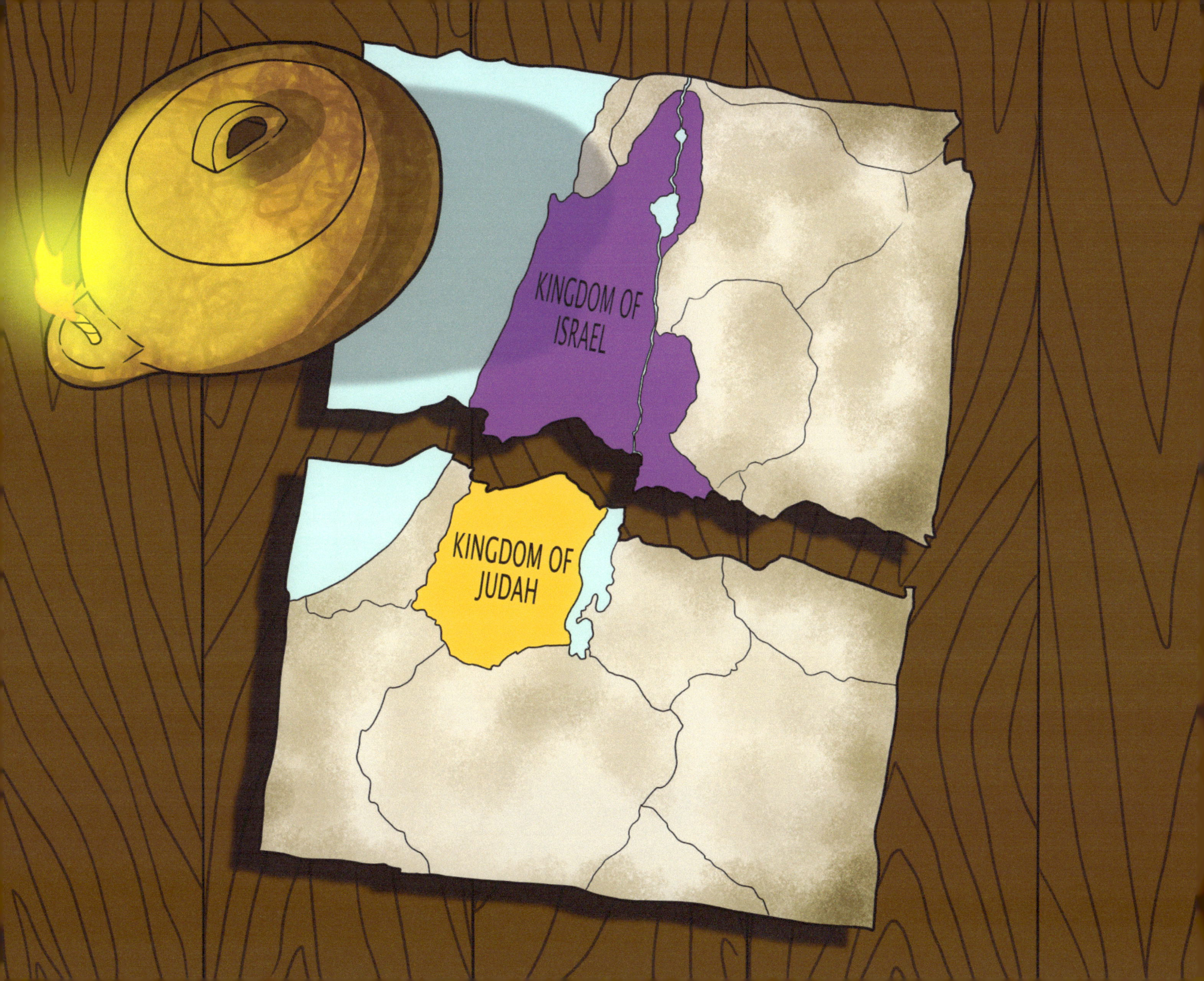

TEST YOUR KNOWLEDGE!

(Match the question with the answer at the bottom of the page)

QUESTIONS

Why did the Queen of Sheba visit Solomon? ....

What gifts did the queen bring with her? ....

How did the queen describe Solomon's servants? ....

What impressed the queen about Solomon? ....

What did the Queen of Sheba say about God in 1 Kings 10:9? ....

In which city was the temple? ....

Who was Solomon's mother? ....

What did Solomon do with the wood that Hiram brought him? ....

What gifts did Solomon give the queen? ....

After the queen and her servants left Jerusalem, where did they go? ....

ANSWERS

1. To test Solomon with difficult questions
2. Camels carrying spices, gold and precious stones
3. Happy
4. Solomon's palace, servants, food, his wisdom, and temple offerings
5. Blessed be Adonai, your God.
6. Jerusalem
7. Bathsheba
8. Make pillars for the temple and palace, and musical instruments
9. Everything she desired
10. They went back home

Complete the Word Search Puzzle

- SOLOMON
- QUEEN
- KING
- TEMPLE
- SHEBA
- ANOINT
- DONKEY
- WISDOM
- CEDAR
- JERUSALEM

```
T W E M M D K V J R
E D I C O V I N E R
M Y O S W F G Y R C
P P D N D Q U K U E
L N V K K O A I S D
E W T P B E M N A A
A N O I N T Y G L R
C S O L O M O N E J
S H E B A Q V W M C
T Q U E E N X M N T
```

Bible Pathway Adventures®

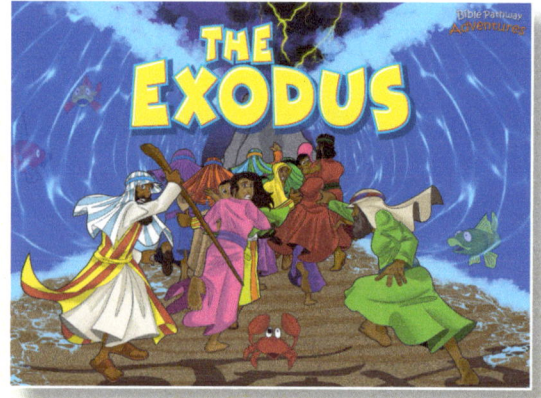

Swallowed by a Fish
Birth of the King
Betrayal of the King
The Risen King
Saved by a Donkey
Thrown to the Lions
Sold into Slavery
The Great Flood
The Chosen Bride
Shipwrecked!
Escape from Egypt
The Exodus
Facing the Giant
Samson

Discover more Bible Pathway Adventures' Bible stories!

Check out Bible Pathway Adventures' Activity Books

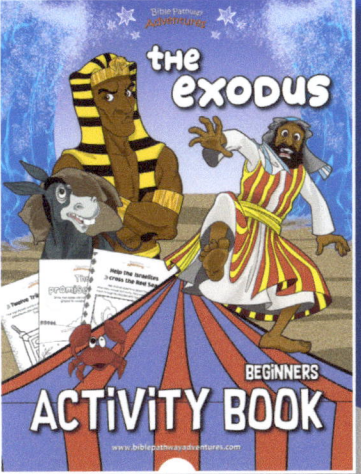
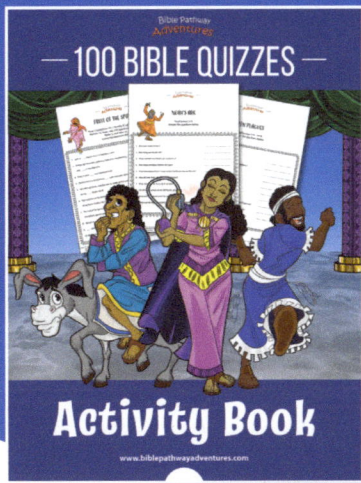

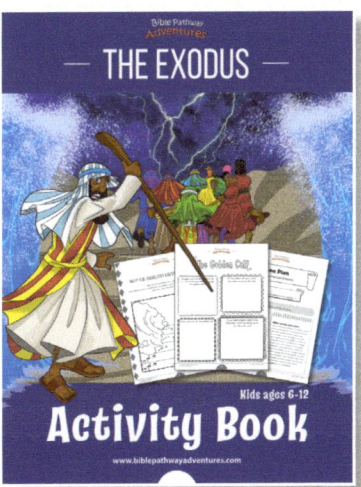

GO TO

www.biblepathwayadventures.com

www.ingramcontent.com/pod-product-compliance
Lightning Source LLC
Chambersburg PA
CBHW040319100526
44583CB00004BB/159